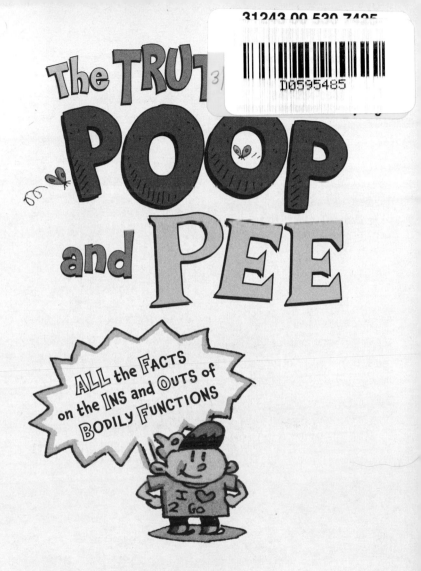

The TRUTH ~~about~~ POOP and PEE

ALL the FACTS on the INS and OUTS of BODILY FUNCTIONS

I ♥ 2 Go

by Susan E. Goodman

illustrated by Elwood H. Smith

PUFFIN BOOKS
An Imprint of Penguin Group (USA)

Rather than using real poop to test toilets, manufacturers use brown fermented beancurd. It looks—and can clog—just like the real thing!

Beaver poop often floats, because it contains so much undigested wood.

Sharks produce spiral poop.

When forced off their nests, eider ducks poop on their eggs to make them less appealing to predators.

Native American Lakota used the ashes from burned poop as toothpaste.

If food is scarce, young cockroaches can live by eating their parents' poop.

Food can remain in your body for up to two days before you poop it out.

On average, people use the toilet five times a day (once to poop, four times to pee). During Operation Desert Storm in 1990, the U.S. military used toilet paper to camouflage their tanks.

Ancient Egyptian tombs had special toilet chambers for the pharaohs to use on their way to the afterlife.

Companies used to test their diapers by using mashed potatoes or peanut butter as a poop substitute.

One of nature's best ways to scatter the seeds of fruit trees is through the droppings of birds and animals that eat the fruit.

Scat, dung, and droppings are all general words for animal poop. There's also deer fewmets, cattle tath, otter spraints, cow flops or pats, buffalo bodewash, and bat guano.

The poop produced while people are fasting has little to no smell.

English king Henry the Eighth had a toileting stool covered with black velvet and studded with 2,000 gold nails.

During the American Revolution, English people jokingly hung portraits of George Washington in their bathrooms, since fear is supposed to help you poop.

Thomas Jefferson had an indoor bathroom at his home, Monticello, and servants hauled away his dirty chamber pots with a system of pulleys.

The ancient Romans had a goddess named Cloacina, who was in charge of toilets and sewers.

The average age for being toilet-trained in the United States is three years old.

Artist Michelangelo bathed some of his statues in donkey dung to make them look older.

In the ancient Roman city of Ephesus, rich citizens sent their slaves to the public bathrooms to warm up the cold marble toilet seats for them.

Many cultures used to try to get rid of freckles by rubbing dung on them.

One jokester in the 1920s made a toilet seat that played the National Anthem whenever people sat down—forcing them to stand up again.

The horses towing carts around Chinese cities must wear "butt bags" to keep the streets clean.

When they are upset, chimps who have been taught sign language indicate their frustration by making the sign for poop.

PUFFIN BOOKS
Published by the Penguin Group
Penguin Group (USA) LLC
375 Hudson Street
New York, New York 10014

USA * Canada * UK * Ireland * Australia
New Zealand * India * South Africa * China

penguin.com
A Penguin Random House Company

This omnibus edition first published in the United States of America by Puffin Books,
an imprint of Penguin Young Readers Group, 2014

The Truth About Poop: First published in the United States of America by Viking,
a division of Penguin Young Readers Group, 2004
Gee Whiz: It's All About Pee: First published in the United States of America by Viking,
a division of Penguin Young Readers Group, 2006

THE LIBRARY OF CONGRESS HAS CATALOGED THE VIKING EDITION OF *THE TRUTH ABOUT POOP* AS FOLLOWS:

Goodman, Susan E., date-
The truth about poop / by Susan E. Goodman ; illustrated by Elwood H. Smith.
p. cm.
Summary: A compendium of fascinating, weird, and gross facts about excrement.
ISBN: 0-670-03674-9 (hardcover)
1. Feces—Juvenile literature. [1. Feces.] I. Smith, Elwood H., date- ill. II. Title.
QP159.G665 2004   612.3'6—dc22   2003022547

THE LIBRARY OF CONGRESS HAS CATALOGED THE VIKING EDITION OF
GEE WHIZ: IT'S ALL ABOUT PEE AS FOLLOWS:

Goodman, Susan E., date-
Gee Whiz! It's all about pee / by Susan E. Goodman ; illustrated by Elwood H. Smith.
p. cm.
Includes bibliographical references.
ISBN: 0-670-06064-X (hardcover)
I. Urine—Juvenile literature. I. Smith, Elwood H., date- ill. II. Title.
QP211.G575 2006
612.4'61—dc22
2006001957

Puffin Books ISBN 978-0-14-751037-2

Printed in the United States of America

1 3 5 7 9 10 8 6 4 2

ACKNOWLEDGMENTS:

It takes a lot of help to do a book like this one. Thanks to all the experts who gave me the straight poop on their specialties, including Jim Fuchs, formerly captain in the U.S. Air Force, Joyce Jatko of the National Science Foundation, Dr. Andrew Jones of York Archaeological Trust, Randy Morgan at the Cincinnati Zoo, Donald Rethke a.k.a. Dr. Flush, and Athos Bousvaros, Lenny Rappaport, and Ed Tronick of Children's Hospital Boston. A special thanks to Elizabeth Law for her sense of humor and editorial style, Teresa Kietlinski and Jim Hoover for their great layout, copyeditor Janet Pascal for keeping me from embarrassing myself, and Elwood H. Smith, whose illustrations are just so much fun.

A book chockful of research requires the help and expertise of so many people. Thanks to Jelle Atema of the Boston University Marine Program, author and reader David Elliott, Dr. Jeffrey L. Forgeng of Higgins Armory Museum, Melanie Kim at Boston Medical Center, Veterinarian Sara Levine, Randy Morgan at the Cincinnati Zoo, Dr. Donald Rethke and others at NASA, Colonel David Snell of the U.S. Air Force, Leslie J. Stein at Monell Chemical Senses Center, and Gary Uhl of American Standard. Tobin Anderson had the best idea for a title. A special thanks to the people at Viking—Jill Davis, who enthusiastically welcomed the idea; Janet Pascal, who so ably shepherded it through each stage; and Jim Hoover, who, once again, showcased my words and Elwood's illustrations to their best advantage.   —S. E. G.

CONTENTS

INTRODUCTION

We eat every day. And we talk a lot about food. We get dressed every day. And we talk a lot about clothes.

WE POOP EVERY DAY, TOO.
But once we're old enough to do it by ourselves, we go into the bathroom and close the door. End of discussion.

It's time to take poop **OUT OF THE CLOSET**. While we're pretending it doesn't exist, amazing things are happening in the poop department.

DID YOU KNOW...

You can be a **BATHROOM PICASSO**.

Eating red meat will make your poop turn darker. Eating beets will make it red. Milk gives it a yellowish tinge, and blackberries can turn it green.

A skipper caterpillar is just an inch and a half long, but it can **SHOOT ITS POOP** a distance of six feet. This Brazilian caterpillar isn't practicing for basketball tryouts. The smell of its poop would tell hungry animals that dinner is near. So the caterpillar protects itself by flicking its feces as far away as possible.

Caterpillars aren't the only ones who should be careful. The navy suggests that people who are stranded at sea should store their **POOP IN THE LIFE RAFT.** Sharks can smell their prey's poop over a mile away.

KNOWING ABOUT POOP CAN SAVE YOUR LIFE.

And that's just the beginning. . . .

BIRDS DO IT, BEES DO IT

EVERYBODY POOPS

The simplest animals—like **JELLYFISH** and **SEA ANEMONES**—have a digestive system with only **ONE OPENING.** Their mouths do double duty—taking food in and pushing waste out. Clearly, having a system with a separate exit is a big improvement.

Animals with this "separate exit" use it in amazing ways. **TURKEY VULTURES,** for example, poop all over their own legs—and not because they have lousy aim. The evaporation of their mostly liquid poop keeps them cool on hot days.

CAMELS live in the desert and can't waste the precious water in their bodies on poop. Their droppings come out so dry that you could strike a match and burn them.

Unlike turkey vultures, **BATS** don't like to poop on themselves. But avoiding it isn't so easy when you hang upside down all day. So bats twist into special pooping postures to keep clean. (Some get dirty anyway. Fruit bats roost in trees, and only the group's "top" bats get to hang—clear and clean—in the highest branches.)

HOW MUCH?/HOW OFTEN?

RABBITS produce an impressive 500 pellets a day. Each of these brown balls is pretty small, but so is the rabbit.

HORSES can lift their tails and unload ten pounds' worth at a time—often without even breaking step.

Scientists recently found a chunk of fossilized **TYRANNOSAURUS REX DUNG** that weighed a whopping **16 POUNDS.** By studying this 17-inch, 65-million-year-old piece of paleo-plop, they learned that T. rex wasn't a careful eater. It barely chewed cow-sized dinosaurs enough to crush their bones before swallowing.

A **GOOSE** is a living poop factory. Food goes in one end and then . . . Geese poop, on average, once every 12 minutes.

SLOTHS, on the other hand, do everything slowly. They eat slowly. They digest their food ten times more slowly than a cow. They even poop slowly. Once a week, sloths, who do everything else in the treetops, slowly climb down to the ground to poop. They make the most of that trip. Sloths can poop out two pounds of waste in a single session—over a quarter of what they weigh.

While they're hibernating, **BEARS** don't poop at all. Their bodies create an internal plug made from feces, old cells, and hair that keeps them from pooping during their winter sleep.

DROPPED DROPPINGS

When we need to poop, we look for a bathroom. We're not the only ones. **ANTS** in New Guinea go to nubs on the branches of a special vine. As a reward to the plant for providing these perfectly shaped ant toilets, the ant poop rots into food for the vine's airborne roots.

LLAMA herds set up a "bathroom" area and wait their turns to use it. **WILDEBEESTS** grazing on the African plains also create a separate place to relieve themselves. This plan keeps fresh manure away from their dinner. It also fertilizes a new patch of grass for a future meal.

NAKED MOLE-RATS (which have been described as looking like hot-dogs left in the microwave too long) live in eastern Africa in huge maze-like underground towns. Their special toilet chambers aren't designed simply to keep the rest of their burrows clean. Mole-rats regularly go in there to roll in their own poop. Strange taste in perfume? Not really. Mole-rat colonies have up to 300 members. The smell of their group's poop helps them distin-guish between family and foe if a fight breaks out with another colony.

DUNG DISPATCH

Without telephones and e-mail at their disposal, some animals use poop—at least the smell of it—to get their messages across.

The dung from a **MOTHER HORSE,** for example, says, "Here I am." The smell of her poop is one way her foal can find her.

A male **BLACK-FOOTED SALAMANDER**'s poop also says, "Here I am"—but to a different audience. Female salamanders take a whiff to figure out what kind of food he has eaten. If he has eaten well, chances are he is strong and fit and will be a good father for their children.

When **WOLVERINES** are done feeding on a dead animal, they save the rest for later by pooping all over it.

What's the message? "This is mine, don't touch!"

AFTER THAT, WHO WOULD WANT TO?

The smell of **LION DUNG** would shout, "I'm here," too—something lions want to hide from their prey. That's why lions cover this evidence whenever they are on the prowl (a habit house-cats carry over in their litterboxes).

POOP WARFARE

It's a dog-eat-dog, bug-eat-bug world out there. And poop is often a **WEAPON** in the war. Some animals use it to trap dinner, others to avoid being dinner themselves.

It hardly seems fair—the **ASSASSIN BUG,** who loves the taste of termites, uses the termites' own droppings to trap them. It covers its back with termite poop and waits for the next poor termite looking for a toilet.

Hunters aren't the only ones to use poop camouflage. The **TORTOISE BEETLE LARVA** starts eating as soon as it is hatched. It starts pooping shortly afterward, in golden strands, which it weaves into a shield. It munches on, hiding from enemies in its new poop-tent.

The **JAEGER** uses its poop as a weapon, not a disguise. Get too close to its nest of chicks and you'll find out how. Like any good fighter pilot, this seabird flies close to its target, then . . . bombs away!

The **CRAB SPIDER** in New Guinea doesn't have to work so hard. Its coloring makes it look like bird droppings. When it's hungry, the spider sits on a leaf and splashes some extra white silk around to perfect its disguise as bird splat. The owlet moth that tries to sip a little salt from these droppings gets a deadly surprise.

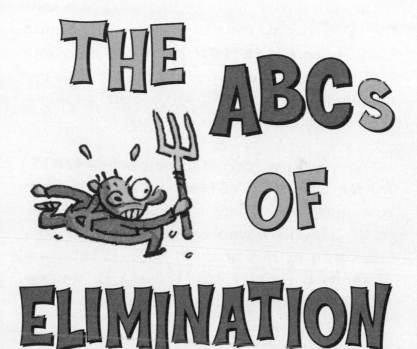

THE ABCs OF ELIMINATION

BY PROCESS OF ELIMINATION

The eating part might be over when you leave the table, but you're hardly done with dinner. That's when **DIGESTION** kicks into gear. Your stomach starts churning, turning the food into nutritious goo. Most of it will be used as fuel to keep you going.

The rest is transferred to your body's **WASTE MANAGEMENT SYSTEM.** It travels through your intestines, where it meets up with other trash your body wants to get rid of. It combines with extra water, old used-up cells, and unwanted bacteria. Lots of bacteria. On average, we poop out 100 billion bacteria a day.

The end of your intestines, the **COLON,** is like a waiting room. Poop gathers there until you feel that "urge to purge" and go to the bathroom. Generally, the more you eat, the more you poop. What you eat makes a difference, too. High fiber foods like vegetables create bigger stools. So does eating raw foods. Lots of meat and completely cooked foods produce smaller, darker ones.

To know what's big and what's small, you have to know what is normal. On average, people produce about an **OUNCE OF POOP FOR EACH 12 POUNDS OF BODY WEIGHT**. So a 96-pound kid might flush away a half-pound of poop in a single session.

HISTORY OF THE TOILET: PART I

In our part of the world, most people have flush toilets. But it took a lot of history to get this far. . . .

Long, long ago, people roamed the fields and forests and didn't have to keep things tidy. Once they started settling into **VILLAGES**, let alone cities, they had to figure out where to put their mess. From the beginning, smart people realized that using water to wash away waste was the goal. Even 4,500 years ago, one Asian culture poured water into their toilets so the contents would travel through chutes into an outside drainage system.

Medieval times in Europe were called **"THE DARK AGES"** for many reasons. Toiletwise, they remembered water, but forgot the plumbing. The toilets in some stone castles emptied out of tiny windows or long chutes into a hole in the ground—or a river if one was nearby.

Around this time, people said that London Bridge was built "for wise men to go over and fools to go under." Maybe the **PUBLIC BATHROOMS** located on the bridge had something to do with it. They emptied into the river below.

In 1596, **SIR JOHN HARINGTON** actually designed a flush toilet. But in 1596, buildings had no plumbing to bring in the water that makes a flush toilet flush. So people kept pooping in outhouses or inside in **CHAMBER POTS** and throwing the results out of windows onto city streets. And the flush toilet had to wait another few hundred years to become a welcome fixture in our bathrooms.

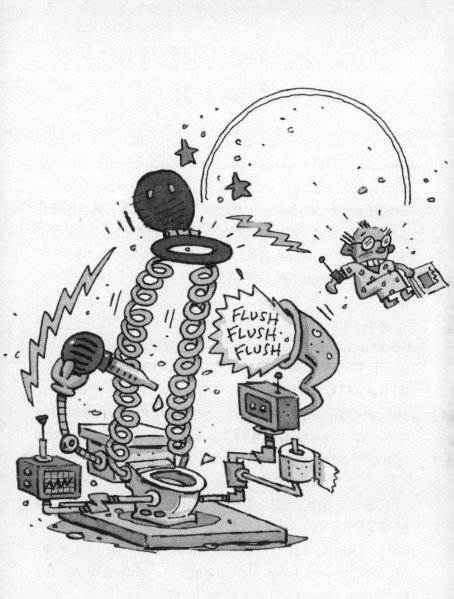

HISTORY OF THE TOILET: PART II

Once cities had sewer systems and bathrooms moved indoors (starting about 1850), the flush toilet's time had come. People like to think that British plumber **THOMAS CRAPPER** invented the flush toilet. He certainly had the best name for the job. And he did create a few of its improvements.

But many people pitched in to produce this all-important invention. One developed the first good **FLUSH MECHANISM**. Another made a **CERAMIC BOWL**, which was cleaner than the old wood or metal ones. Still another created a system to keep **OUTSIDE SEWER SMELLS** from traveling through the toilet into the house.

Toilets are still improving. Americans put **MOTORS** in some of them, adding power to each flush. The U.S. "Peacekeeper" reinforces Mom's lesson about putting the seat down—it's the only way to flush this model.

But the Japanese are the real winners of the Toilet Super Bowl. Press a button and some Japanese toilets make the sound of flushing water to hide more embarrassing sounds. Others have a kind of **EJECTION SEAT** for older people who can't stand back up without help.

One Japanese company makes a **"SMART TOILET"** that takes your temperature and blood pressure and can send this information to your doctor's office. One button on the **WASHLET TOILET** controls the temperature of the water that washes your backside. Another operates the blow-dry feature. This model is very expensive, but at least its owners save on toilet paper.

THE WORLD PRE-T.P.

There was a **WORLD BEFORE TOILET PAPER** and much of it wasn't pretty. Or comfortable.

Throughout history, wipers have reached for nearby objects. **LEAVES** were popular. **STONES** too, preferably smooth ones. Eskimos grabbed **MOSS** or **SNOW** depending on the season. Some people on the American coasts used **MUSSEL SHELLS**, which are actually a very convenient size and shape.

The ancient Roman version of toilet paper was a sponge on a stick sitting in a bucket of salt water. That may sound uncomfortable, but the Ouch Award goes to Spanish sailors who used the frayed end of **OLD ANCHOR CABLES**. Early Hawaiians are runners-up with **COCONUT HUSKS**.

And soon after the Pilgrims learned to grow corn, they figured out what to do with the **COBS**. Corncobs became the American wipe of choice for centuries. Kids were taught to start with red ones, then use a white cob to see if they should continue.

In 1391, the Chinese started producing **PAPER** for wiping purposes—but only for their emperors. These monarchs must have been very clean. Each sheet was three feet across.

The invention of the printing press created other papery possibilities. In a letter, the English nobleman Lord Chesterfield told his son to carry a **CHEAP BOOK OF POETRY** at all times. That way, he'd have something to read on the toilet and a good use for each page he finished.

When **DAILY NEWSPAPERS** became popular in the 1700s, ordinary people could afford to use paper. In the late 1800s, the pages of the Sears catalog hung on nails in outhouses across America, but first, moms tore out the pictures of women's undergarments.

TOILET PAPER
ROLL CALL

By 1857, the printing press, bicycles, and baseball had already been invented. What was left? **TOILET PAPER!** So a New Yorker named **JOSEPH C. GAYETTY** produced the first TP in packs. Five hundred sheets of it sold for 50 cents. His idea was not a success. Evidently people weren't used to "wasting" an empty sheet of paper.

In 1890, the **SCOTT PAPER COMPANY** became the first ones to make toilet paper on rolls. Eventually the idea caught on—big time. A recent survey asked people what they'd want to have if stranded on a desert island. Almost half of them picked toilet paper over food.

Americans do like their toilet paper. On average, we use almost **9 SHEETS** per trip. And 20,805 sheets per year per person, which, when unrolled, would stretch three-quarters of a mile.

Americans use a lot, but Japanese women use more. On average, each one of them goes through about **TWO AND A HALF MILES** of the stuff a year.

Many people in India and Arab countries **DON'T USE TOILET PAPER** at all. They think smearing themselves with paper is a bad way to get clean. They **WIPE WITH THEIR LEFT HAND** instead and wash up with water. Unsurprisingly, they use only their right hand when eating.

WHERE DOES IT GO?

WHAT HAPPENS WHEN YOU FLUSH?

The water swishes out of your toilet into a pipe. If you live in a city, the pipe leads from your basement to a bigger pipe under the street.

SWOOSH!

FLUSH!

There, your poop and paper join up with your neighbors'. Small pipes keep feeding into bigger ones until pipes up to 11 feet across carry rivers of watery waste to a **TREATMENT PLANT**. In

SLOOSH!

TREATMENT CENTER

Boston, for example, it takes more than 54,000 miles of sewers to do the job.

On its journey, your poop mixes in with everything from food that slipped down the kitchen sink to rain and leaves from the **STORM DRAIN**.

At the plant, huge screens filter out big stuff like diapers and branches. Rocks and sand sink to the bottom of tanks and are carted away.

Poop and other solids settle to the bottom of the next tank and get a new name—**SLUDGE**. Some cities dry the sludge and **BURN IT**; others **DUMP IT** in landfills. Still others put it in an airless tank with a type of bacteria that finds it delicious. Whatever the bacteria leave behind is great for fertilizer.

In fact, when the city of Milwaukee, Wisconsin, realized this, they went into business.

Today, Milorganite (**MIL**waukee **ORGA**nic **NIT**rog**E**n) is a top-selling fertilizer for golf courses, which means that putting greens everywhere are just a little greener thanks to the poop from Milwaukee.

EXTREME POOP

There are wild places on this planet far away from regular plumbing.

WHAT HAPPENS WHEN WE POOP THERE?

Disposal in the Amazon rain forest is not a problem, as one scientist discovered when he deposited a sample on the jungle floor. Within minutes, beetles and bees found this **TASTY TREAT**. Within a few hours, it had totally disappeared.

Getting rid of the stuff takes a lot longer at South Pole Station in Antarctica, where the average temperature is about −50°F. There, scientists use toilets placed over deep holes drilled into the icecap. The icecap is always moving seaward, so the poop and pee **GO ALONG FOR THE RIDE**. Today's wad of waste will reach the ocean in about 100,000 years.

High in the Andes Mountains, mothers carry babies on their backs, wrapped in cloth slings. These tots spend much of their day **LYING IN POOP** and pee and actually **GROW FASTER** because of it. At 12,000 feet above sea level, it is cold, dry, and harder to breathe. Being closed in with the waste creates a warm, humid space. So the babies can put their energy into growing instead of staying warm.

In survival training, soldiers are taught to **LIE ON POOP**, too. Experts say that dry cowpats—with a little give in the center—make a great bed. Line them up and cover them with a poncho in case one is still too "soft." Warmed up by a soldier's body, they keep the heat all night long.

WASTE IN SPACE

Graduating from diapers is a big deal for little kids. But if you become an astronaut, you may have to start wearing them again. Astronauts on spacewalks wear disposable diapers, because they're outside, away from a toilet, for up to seven hours. Since grownups don't like to think they are wearing diapers, they call them **"MAXIMUM ABSORPTION GARMENTS."**

Inside the ship, things are more problematic. In weightless conditions, anything loose—food scraps, stray pens, blobs of water—will float around the cabin. So good **WASTE DISPOSAL** is very important.

Take the rats, for example, that are part of science experiments. NASA wants the **RATS** to fly in space without their turds flying around the shuttle. During missions, steady streams of air flow through the rat cages. They push the poop and pee into waste trays and keep them there until the end of the flight.

Astronauts pee into a funnel, and gentle suction transfers the urine into a **HOLDING TANK**. The same kind of suction moves their poop into another tank. But pooping into a space toilet is complicated. Astronauts must swing bars across their legs to stay put.

Why? Gravity is one scientific law to worry about in space. **NEWTON'S THIRD LAW** is another. It says that every action has an equal and opposite reaction. When astronauts use their muscles to poop, they create a downward push.

The equal and opposite reaction? Without being held down, the astronauts would shoot **UP, UP, AND AWAY!**

USEFUL POOP

USEFUL POOP

We call it a waste product, but . . . ancient Romans used pigeon poop to **BLEACH** their hair. And many expert gardeners insist that ZooDoo, made from elephant and rhino dung, is the **WORLD'S BEST FERTILIZER**.

What can you do with a pile of poop? **PLENTY**.

Today, doctors examine your poop to see if you have certain diseases. In the old days, they gave poop to you as **MEDICINE** instead.

Hawk poop, lamb poop, **CROCODILE POOP**—they rubbed it on you, mixed it into food, or made a tea out of it to cure everything from dandruff to deafness.

Termites mix their poop with chewed-up wood to build the huge towers they live in. Secretary birds line their nests with **DRIED ZEBRA DUNG**. The Maasai, an African tribe, mix cow poop with ashes to make the walls of their huts. Luckily, the poop, once dried, doesn't smell at all.

The Bedouins of Qatar don't come across many toilets on their travels through the desert. Even today, they use dried camel pats **TO WIPE** their babies' bottoms.

AND THAT'S NOT ALL...

POOP CLUES

Police use **DOGS** to find missing people. Now scientists use them too—to sniff out the poop of wild animals. Scientists can learn a great deal about bears from their scat, for example, without ever bothering the animal itself. By looking at the DNA in poop, they can figure out which bear made it and which other bears it's related to.

PALEONTOLOGISTS learn about the past through fossils, including chunks of fossilized poop called coprolites. One scientist analyzed a piece made 20,000 years ago by a **GIANT GROUND SLOTH** in Nevada.

By figuring out what this 1,000-pound animal ate, he also learned more about the climate back then. Now a **DESERT**, this area must have been very different then to grow the sloth's diet of grass, lilies, and grapes.

English scientist **ANDREW JONES** studied what Vikings ate by looking at their coprolites. But first he had to figure out which poop fossils actually belonged to the

Vikings and not their pigs or dogs. To solve the problem, Dr. Jones put his own digestive tract to work. He copied the Vikings by eating lots of fish, bones and all. So did the dogs and pigs in his laboratory. Once he saw how leftover fish bones looked in his own poop versus fresh dog or pig poop, he could identify which of the fossilized stuff came from humans. The Vikings, by the way, also ate their share of beef and vegetables.

Humans aren't the only poop detectives. Small **WOLF SPIDERS** know when big, dangerous wolf spiders are near, by detecting chemicals in their poop. Then they move around much more carefully.

Acme Buffalo Chips
DRIED & READY TO BURN!
3 MILES AHEAD

POOP POWER

Pioneers on the prairie didn't have trees or coal to burn as fuel. So settlers burned **DRIED BUFFALO CHIPS** to keep their houses warm.

Poop as fuel did not end with buffalo chips. In rural India, they use **"COW CHIPS."** Fresh cow manure is patted into round discs and stuck on walls to dry. As soon as it has dried enough to fall off the wall, it's ready to burn. India burns one quarter of all the dung its cows produce. That's fuel for 330 million people.

When poop gets old and breaks down without any oxygen around, part of it turns to gas. One out of every ten people on Earth burns this **POOP-GAS**, or bio-gas, as fuel. It actually makes a lot of sense. In the country of Nepal, for example, the poop-gas from two cows provides enough cooking fuel for a family of six.

Poop might even power our trips to **OTHER PLANETS**. NASA is studying how to burn food scraps, space garbage, and astronaut poop (along with regular fuel) to power a spaceship to Mars.

POOP AS FOOD

Cooking with poop is one thing but . . . **EATING IT**?

It might not sound so tasty to you, but many bugs search high and (mostly) low for a **DROPPINGS DINNER**. Up to one hundred different kinds of insects have been found dining on a single cowpat. Tumblebugs love the stuff. They roll their eggs in a ball of dung so their newly hatched babies will have a ready food supply.

When a dog chows down, however, it's usually to get a helping of bacteria. These tiny organisms move from the poop into the animal's gut. There, they help break down the new food that comes their way. That's why baby vampire bats polish off their parents' poop—they're **GOBBLING UP BACTERIA** needed to digest their special diet of blood.

Rabbits do it for a different reason. Just like cattle, rabbits eat plants that are really **HARD TO DIGEST**. A cow's stomachs let her bring food up again so she can break it down by chewing it twice. A rabbit can't do this. Eating its own poop gives the rabbit a second chance to get nourishment from its food.

POOP GAMES

When you want to **PLAY** outside, you might grab a ball or a Frisbee. The pioneers on the prairie had to make their own fun. Sometimes when gathering **DRIED BUFFALO POOP** for fuel, they competed to see who could toss the most chips into the wagon without breaking them.

Today, the rules are a little different at the annual World Championship **COW CHIP THROW** in Oklahoma. Chips must be at least six inches across. Wearing gloves isn't allowed. But licking your fingers for a better grip is legal. Contestants have two chances to throw these **"BROWN FRISBEES"** as far as possible. It's not all that far,

by the way. The best throw
ever is just about 16 feet.

Poop travels much
farther at the **MOOSE
DROPPING FESTIVAL** in
Talkeetna, Alaska. There
people buy numbered moose
nuggets that are carried up
1,000 feet by weather bal-
loon. At 6 p.m, a cord
is pulled and it rains
moose poop. The owner
of the nugget that falls
closest to the X drawn on
the ground wins $1,000.

POOP PRESENTS

At the Moose Dropping Festival, people can buy **MOOSE POOP GIFTS** to bring home. Want a moose drop keychain? Or a mug with turds glued to its bottom? How about shiny brown buttons to sew on your sweater? Then there's the Poop Moose. Lift its tail and M&Ms drop out of its behind.

POOP ARTISTS in Alaska dry and paint moose droppings so they're hard and odor-free.

In Japan, they heat and press city sewage (a nice name for human poop) until it turns into something like brown stone. They use this **"METRO-MARBLE"** in necklaces and earrings.

A male **DUNG BEETLE** doesn't dress up the poop he gives to his girlfriend. He just uses his oversized fangs to make a big ball of it, one about 30 times her size. If she likes her gift, she climbs on top and he rolls off with her for a little romance.

DANGEROUS POOP

So far we've talked about poop as useful. Sometimes it's anything but. If you look up in most cities, pigeons are dripping white caps onto statues' heads, or adding polka dots to their robes. Pigeon droppings contain acid, which eats away at buildings, statues, wood, and car paint. Some cities are fighting back. London has outlawed selling pigeon food. And Venice has mixed birth control into its pigeon feed.

DO NOT FEED PIGEONS

Pig manure is an even greater hazard—especially since there's so much of it (pigs produce four times more poop than humans). Some of its gases can eat through metal. And if a pig poops in a very hot place without enough air circulation, one gas in its poop (hydrogen sulfide) can actually kill it on the spot.

Certain scientists, however, discovered a way to use poop—at least the smell of it—to avoid killing anyone. Instead of firing guns to break up a crowd, a company called M2 Technologies suggests tossing in one of its **"POOP CAP-SULES."** The smell is so intense that anyone nearby has to throw up—or run.

During World War II, "poop" really could kill. The British knew that German tank drivers fighting in the desert thought it was good

luck to drive over camel dung. So they made
EXPLOSIVES that looked exactly like the stuff.
One pass over the poop—and the tanks were out
of action.

German command ordered the drivers
to avoid any dung, but superstitions are hard to
give up. The Brits knew this and made mines
that looked like dung squished by tank tracks.
Drivers thought they were safe and . . .

AFTERWORD—
THE POOP ON POOP

There's a secret every nonfiction writer knows ... research is fun. To write other books, I have paddled the Amazon River and shivered near the North Pole. For this one, I didn't do much hands-on research—thank goodness. But I did learn from personal experience how beets affect poop (page 4).

Mostly I read detailed, often scientific, books on the subject, including:

- *Merde* by Ralph A. Lewin, published by Random House in 1999.
- *The RE/Search Guide to Bodily Fluids* by Paul Spinrad, published by Juno Books in 1994.
- *Cacas: The Encyclopedia of Poo* by Oliviero Toscani, published by Evergreen in 1998.

Doing research can be a treasure hunt. No matter what question you have, someone somewhere has spent a lifetime thinking about the answer. Find that person and you've won the prize.

The treasures I found this time include Dr. Donald Rethke. He helped design space toilets for NASA (page 46)—and goes by the nickname Dr. Flush. Joyce Jatko at the National Science Foundation told me about poop at the South Pole (page 42). She also mentioned that sea urchins use toilet paper flushed into the sea from an Antarctic science center to drape themselves with as camouflage. I asked Dr. Andrew Jones if his experiment with poop (page 55) changed his eating habits. He said no, but he washes his hands much more often now. People who work with poop for a living have a great sense of humor.

IF YOU WANT TO DO A LITTLE RESEARCH OF YOUR OWN, YOU MIGHT TRY READING:

- *The Scoop on Poop* by Wayne Lynch, published by Fifth House in 2002.
- *Grossology* by Sylvia Branzei, published by Price Stern Sloan in 2002.

Or visit the website **www.theplumber.com**.

Rather than using real poop to test toilets, manufacturers use brown fermented beancurd. It looks—and can clog—just like the real thing!

Beaver poop often floats, because it contains so much undigested wood.

Sharks produce spiral poop.

When forced off their nests, eider ducks poop on their eggs to make them less appealing to predators.

Native American Lakota used the ashes from burned poop as toothpaste.

If food is scarce, young cockroaches can live by eating their parents' poop.

Food can remain in your body for up to two days before you poop it out.

On average, people use the toilet five times a day (once to poop, four times to pee). During Operation Desert Storm in 1990, the U.S. military used toilet paper to camouflage their tanks.

Ancient Egyptian tombs had special toilet chambers for the pharaohs to use on their way to the afterlife.

Companies used to test their diapers by using mashed potatoes or peanut butter as a poop substitute.

One of nature's best ways to scatter the seeds of fruit trees is through the droppings of birds and animals that eat the fruit.

Scat, dung, and droppings are all general words for animal poop. There's also deer fewmets, cattle tath, otter spraints, cow flops or pats, buffalo bodewash, and bat guano.

The poop produced while people are fasting has little to no smell.

English king Henry the Eighth had a toileting stool covered with black velvet and studded with 2,000 gold nails.

During the American Revolution, English people jokingly hung portraits of George Washington in their bathrooms, since fear is supposed to help you poop.

Thomas Jefferson had an indoor bathroom at his home, Monticello, and servants hauled away his dirty chamber pots with a system of pulleys.

The ancient Romans had a goddess named Cloacina, who was in charge of toilets and sewers.

The average age for being toilet-trained in the United States is three years old.

Artist Michelangelo bathed some of his statues in donkey dung to make them look older.

In the ancient Roman city of Ephesus, rich citizens sent their slaves to the public bathrooms to warm up the cold marble toilet seats for them.

Many cultures used to try to get rid of freckles by rubbing dung on them.

One jokester in the 1920s made a toilet seat that played the National Anthem whenever people sat down—forcing them to stand up again.

The horses towing carts around Chinese cities must wear "butt bags" to keep the streets clean.

When they are upset, chimps who have been taught sign language indicate their frustration by making the sign for poop.

STOP LOOKING UP. DESPITE POPULAR BELIEF, AIRPLANES DO NOT FLUSH "BLUE ICE"—THE CONTENTS OF THEIR TOILETS—OUT INTO THE AIR. IT GOES INTO TANKS THAT CAN ONLY BE OPENED WHEN PLANES ARE ON THE GROUND. • IN COLONIAL AMERICA, WET BABY DIAPERS (KNOWN AS "NAPKINS") WEREN'T ALWAYS WASHED BETWEEN USES BUT WERE JUST PUT BY THE FIRE TO DRY. • MICE CAN RECOGNIZE THEIR ELDERS BY THE SMELL OF THEIR PEE. • ESKIMOS USED TO USE A BUNCH OF GRASS THAT HAD BEEN WETTED WITH URINE TO CLEAN THEIR MOUTHS AFTER EATING. • MOUSE PEE IS SO STINKY, SCIENTISTS BUILT A SPECIAL MOUSE HOUSE SO ASTRONAUTS COULD BRING MICE INTO SPACE. THE UNIT CAN CONTROL THE ODORS FOR TWENTY-ONE DAYS. TO BE SAFE, NASA ONLY ALLOWS MICE UP THERE FOR SEVENTEEN. • CRANE OPERATORS BUILDING SKYSCRAPERS CAN'T CLIMB DOWN HUNDREDS OF FEET TO PEE. EACH MORNING THEY GO INTO THEIR CABINS WITH A LUNCH PAIL AND A DIFFERENT KIND OF BUCKET. THEY SPEND THEIR DAY EMPTYING ONE AND FILLING THE OTHER. • ZOOKEEPERS IN CALCUTTA, INDIA, WERE CAUGHT DRUGGING RHINOS TO MAKE THEM PEE MORE. THEY SOLD THE URINE TO PEOPLE FOR MEDICINE. • IN 1669, HENNIG BRANDT DISCOVERED PHOSPHORUS, THE THIRTEENTH ELEMENT, WHILE DOING EXPERIMENTS WITH URINE. • SCIENTISTS ARE GENETICALLY ALTERING MICE SO THEY CAN GROW HUMAN DRUGS IN THEIR BLADDERS AND PEE IT OUT. • PEOPLE WHO WORK OUTSIDE, LIKE FISHERMEN AND LUMBERJACKS, SOMETIMES PEE ON THEIR HANDS TO WARM THEM. • IN AFRICA, FARMERS

SPRAY COW PEE ON COTTON PLANTS, AND IT KEEPS THE BUGS AWAY. IF IT DRIPS INTO THE SOIL, IT WORKS AS FERTILIZER TOO. • ROMANS USED URINE AS A MOUTH-WASH AND TOOTH CLEANER. • IN JAPAN, URINE USED TO BE SOLD TO FARMERS TO BE MADE INTO FER-TILIZER. • IN ANCIENT MEXICO, AZTEC DOCTORS HAD PATIENTS DRINK URINE TO RELIEVE STOMACH PROB-LEMS. • SOME OF THE WORDS FOR TOILET INCLUDE THE CAN, JOHN, FLUSHER, HEAD, LATRINE, POT, THRONE, DOINGS, NECESSARIUM, AND THE HOLY OF HOLIES. • WOMEN TAKE THREE TIMES AS LONG IN THE BATH-ROOM AS MEN. • A JAPANESE COMPANY HAS CREATED A TOILET THAT PLAYS ONE OF SIX SOUNDTRACKS WHEN IN USE, INCLUDNG RUSHING WATER AND BIRDSONG. • URINE HELPS CONTRIBUTE TO GREENHOUSE GASES, SO THE NEW ZEALAND GOVERNMENT WANTED TO TAX FARMERS FOR EACH COW AND SHEEP THEY OWNED. THE LAW DIDN'T PASS. • IN ONE VOODOO CURSE, A BOTTLE IS FILLED WITH PINS, NEEDLES, NAILS, "EVIL" HERBS, AND THE VICTIM'S URINE; THEN IT'S WEDGED IN A HOLE IN A TREE WHERE IT CAN'T BE FOUND. THE VICTIM IS SUPPOSED TO GET KIDNEY DISEASE. • MALE ELEPHANTS FIND OUT IF A FEMALE IS IN THE MOOD FOR ROMANCE BY SNIFFING HER PEE. • IN THE SIXTEENTH CENTURY, THE ENGLISH AND DUTCH USED TO "DRINK FLAPDRAGONS"— TOAST SOMEONE'S HEALTH BY DRINKING URINE. • IN BRAZIL, IN 1963, LONGSHOREMEN WENT ON STRIKE FOR 20 PERCENT "SHAME PAY" WHEN THEY HAD TO UNLOAD TOILETS.

GEE WHIZ!

Pee is a part of our daily lives. And that's a *GOOD THING.*

Imagine what would happen if we didn't pee. All that water and milk, juicy fruit and soup, building up and up until . . . well, it's best not to think about that.

Let's just say that *PEE CAN SAVE YOUR LIFE*—in more ways than one.

Nowadays they use chemicals instead, but not long ago, drug companies used a part of our pee to make medicine. This substance, called urokinase, helped dissolve the blood clots that caused heart attacks.

Pee also gives warning about another kind of attack. While out with their cattle at night, Maasai herdsmen in Africa sometimes wake to what seems like a rainstorm. This downpour is actually the sound of their *ENTIRE HERD* peeing at once. The cattle's fear tells the herdsmen that a lion is about to strike.

In 1815, Captain James Riley and the crew of the *Commerce* were **SHIPWRECKED** off the coast of Africa. To get back home, they had to cross the very hot, very dry Sahara Desert. When they ran out of water, they survived by drinking camel urine.

WE DON'T TALK ABOUT IT MUCH, BUT PEE IS PRETTY AMAZING.

HOW AMAZING?

READ ON....

PEE
BASICS

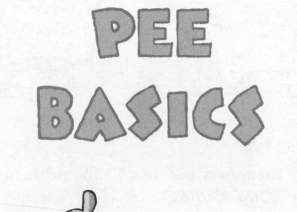

The watery part of food and drink makes a **LONG JOURNEY** before it passes out of your body as urine. It is absorbed into your bloodstream first. Your heart pumps this blood around and around your body, passing it through your kidneys at each turn.

In fact, 400 gallons of blood pass through an adult's kidneys each day, and about 150 gallons for a ten-year-old kid. The kidneys pull out waste products, salt, and about a quart and a half of water a day. This **SOON-TO-BE PEE** then travels to its storage tank—the bladder. Kids' bladders can hold an ounce or more for every year of their age. Adult bladders can store up to 2½ cups of urine. But they feel the urge to pee five to seven times a day, whenever they collect about a cup's worth.

Pee is light or dark yellow depending on the amount of water in it. A mellow yellow turns **NEON BRIGHT,** however, if you take Vitamin B. Beets, rhubarb, and blackberries can turn it reddish brown.

While it's inside you, pee doesn't smell at all. It only gets **STINKY** after it sits out in the air. Some medicines make your pee smell different. Eating asparagus also gives it a funny odor, although only half of us have the gene that lets us detect that perfume.

Talk about **PERFUME**—some women in ancient Rome drank turpentine (which can be poisonous!) because it made their urine smell like roses.

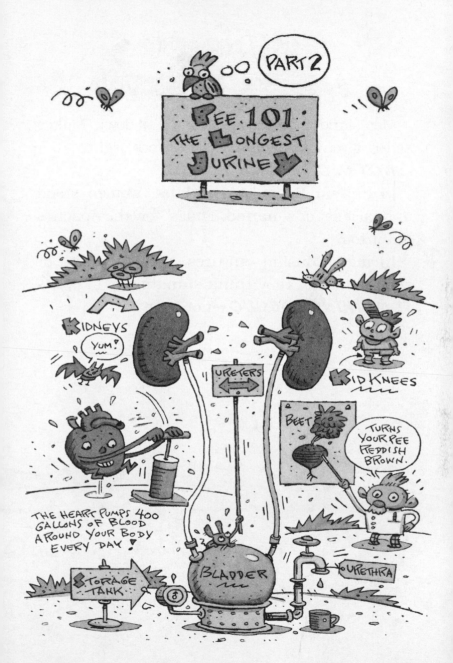

83

STAND UP
AND BE COUNTED

Men stand up to pee and women sit down. Makes sense, given the way our bodies work, right?

NOT NECESSARILY.

In ancient Egypt and Ireland, women stood and men sat or squatted. That's how the Apaches did it too.

In many Muslim cultures, everybody sits or squats. In fact, they think standing up to pee is **SOMETHING DOGS DO**—not humans.

In ancient China, everyone stood. Chinese noblemen peed into hollow canes so the liquid would flow far from their bodies. You would too if you wore such fancy clothes at court.

Until 200 years ago, European women also peed standing up because of their clothes. They wore long dresses and **NO UNDERPANTS.** When necessary, they could stand and pee—hopefully outside—without anyone else noticing.

Sometimes standing up to pee is a mistake. Each year, in Canada, about 225 men stand up in a boat so they can pee over the side—and, as a consequence, **FALL OVERBOARD** and drown.

TO PEE OR NOT TO PEE

Some people's jobs make us wonder: How do they manage to pee?

Take **YE OLDE KNIGHT** in armor, for example. Actually, he didn't have as hard a time as you might think. Wearing a suit of armor was like wearing a short dress, except that it was made of metal and weighed 65 pounds. Its steel plates didn't completely cover his middle. So the knight could pull up his mail skirt and pull down his loosened hose and underwear. He had to be careful, though. The acid in urine could **RUST** his armor.

Knights dealt with their bathroom emergencies before riding into battle. Fighter-jet pilots don't have that luxury. Flying alone, they cannot dash to the toilet (in fact, there isn't one on board!). Luckily, they have baglike gadgets called **PIDDLE-PAKS** to pee into while sitting at their controls.

Truck drivers don't have toilets in their eighteen-wheelers either. They could pull into a rest stop, but sometimes they use their own version of a Piddle-Pak instead. They pee into gallon jugs and toss them on the side of the road. During just one month, cleanup crews in Washington State found over 1,000 of these bottles on a 100-mile stretch of highway. And that's not the worst of it. In the summer's heat, pressure builds up inside these jugs—and they can **EXPLODE** upon contact.

PEEING THROUGH HISTORY

I. PREHISTORY

We know ancient people ate bison and woolly mammoth, because they decorated their caves with pictures of their hunts, and anthropologists have found fossilized animal bones in prehistoric **TRASH HEAPS**. Unfortunately early man never painted pictures of where he went to the bathroom—and pee leaves no fossil evidence. So where prehistoric people peed is a bit of a **MYSTERY**. Most likely, they went outside their caves and camps.

Many animals have special toileting areas, from cats and rabbits to llamas and wildebeests. We can only hope that early humans were as sensible.

II. THE ROMAN EMPIRE

Rome brought civilization to the world in more ways than one. In the first century A.D., the city built grand public bathrooms of polished marble. Each toilet had its own bucket of salt water with a **SPONGE** tied to a stick for wiping. People paid to use these bathrooms; then the city made even more money by selling the pee to tradesmen who bleached cloth with it.

Even ancient Rome had its share of **GRAF-FITI** artists. So officials posted a warning. They adorned the bathrooms with paintings of gods who would punish anyone who wrote on its walls.

III. EUROPE

For more than a thousand years after the Roman Empire fell, Europe went through a bad time toiletwise. Public facilities ranged from none to worse. People on the streets of Edinburgh, Scotland, had to search for the man who patrolled the city with a **BIG BUCKET** and a bigger cloak. For a price, they could use his bucket with the cape draped around them for privacy.

Indoor options weren't much better. In Italy, the artist Leonardo da Vinci proposed that houses be

built with spiral staircases so people couldn't pee in the corners.

In Paris, a thousand people could be entertained in the Louvre, the king's palace. But they did not have a single public bathroom to go to. Countesses, dukes, and admirals all peed (and pooped!) in courtyards, hallways, and empty rooms. Meanwhile, the common folk were throwing the contents of their chamber pots **OUT OF WINDOWS** onto city streets. Pedestrians didn't know whether to protect themselves by looking up or watching where they stepped.

No wonder they had a **REVOLUTION.**

IV. THE WHITE HOUSE

In 1776, the United States had *its* revolution. Its goal of equality may have inspired plans for the **WHITE HOUSE**. The president's plumbing was no better than anyone else's. Even though inventors had started working on toilets by then, the White House was built with only one **OUT-HOUSE** in its backyard.

In 1801, President Thomas Jefferson had two small rooms built, each with a toilet-like device flushed by an overhead tank of rainwater. As time and technology advanced, many toilets were added. For a long time, however, there still weren't enough for all the guests at big dinner parties. After a meal in the late 1800s, gentlemen would go to a private room to smoke cigars and use chamber pots. Women mostly used **CONTROL.**

Nowadays there are thirty-five bathrooms in the White House. There are also hundreds of people working and visiting there during the day. Don't worry about the president, though. He has his own private bathroom, right off the Oval Office.

V. THE FUTURE

It's nighttime and you stumble toward the bathroom, mumbling a few words to let your toilet know you're coming. It turns on a light to welcome you. And turns off the **VIDEO TILES** on the bathroom wall because you're not allowed to watch late-night TV.

Toilets of the future will be very **SMART.** Recognizing voices, they'll raise their seats for boys and put them down for girls. They'll warm that seat for those who want it. They will even adjust themselves to the perfect height for each visitor.

HERE
I COME!

Z

They will wash and dry you if need be—no more toilet paper. Meanwhile their computers will analyze your pee (and poop) to make sure you're healthy. If there's a problem, they can e-mail your doctor. If you aren't eating enough **FRUITS AND VEGETABLES,** they can e-mail the supermarket to deliver some.

Finally, they will flush on command—kids in the future will have no excuse.

PEES IN A (SPACE) POD

America's first manned space flight in 1961 was only fifteen minutes long. So no one worried about toilets. But delays forced astronaut Alan Shepard to sit in the rocket for hours, waiting for takeoff. After a while, he needed to pee. Badly. Shepard became the first American in space and also the first one to **WET HIS SPACESUIT.**

Eventually astronauts got a space toilet. To use it, they each have their own funnel attached to a tube. They can pee into this funnel, nicknamed *"MR. THIRSTY,"* while sitting or standing, even while floating around. A gentle vacuum sucks the urine into a tank without spilling a drop. This is very important since astronauts aren't the only things that can float around the cabin.

When the tank is full, they shoot the pee outside, where it freezes into clouds of ice crystals that look like **STARS.** Astronaut Wally Schirra liked to call it "Constellation Urion."

One time the pee froze onto the spacecraft. Mission Control was afraid it would damage the ship, but the crew balked at the idea of doing a spacewalk to fix it. No one wanted to be known as the astronaut who **CHIPPED PEE OFF THE SHUTTLE.** Eventually they used the ship's robot arm instead.

Bringing water into space is expensive. So the International Space Station is building a system to purify and reuse the water in pee—and not just human pee. Many animal experiments are conducted on board; NASA estimates that **SEVENTY-TWO RATS** pee about as much as one astronaut.

THE CALL OF NATURE

Liquid in, liquid out—the idea behind urination seems pretty simple. But different animals do it in very different ways. . . .

When a **VAMPIRE BAT** taps into dinner, it drinks about two tablespoons of blood. Doesn't seem like much, but this feast equals more than half of the bat's body weight. That's quite a load to lift into the air when the bat flies home.

Luckily, the vampire bat's urinary system works overtime. Two minutes after the bat starts drinking, it starts peeing. It drinks and pees and pees and drinks—keeping the nutritious part of the blood while unloading the watery part. By the time the bat is done with its meal, it has already slimmed down enough for **TAKEOFF.**

Bird pee isn't very watery. Having sort-of **SOLID PEE** isn't that important for birds that are flying or perched in trees. But it is the best pee to have when growing inside an egg. For one thing, it takes up less room in the shell. It also does not dissolve so it can't poison the developing chick.

Baby bears are born in the winter and stay inside their dens until spring. Each time the newborn cubs finish nursing, their mom licks their **BOTTOMS** to make them pee. The mother bear then drinks the pee, which keeps their home clean and tidy.

Mice are little animals. They don't **DRINK** much—or pee much either. It would take a dozen mice one whole day to fill a tablespoon with pee.

Horses are much bigger. A large one, like a Clydesdale, can pee more than 4½ gallons a day.

Elephants are huge, and they pee **HUGE AMOUNTS**—more than 13 gallons a day. But if you want to double-check this measurement, pick a male elephant to follow around. It would just be easier. Female elephants often poop and pee at the same time.

A fin whale's bladder can hold 5½ gallons of urine. The amount of urine it produces each day, however, is a mystery. When an animal pees into the ocean, it's kind of **TOUGH TO MEASURE.**

DRY RUN

In dry climates, water is so **PRECIOUS** that animals can't waste a drop. That includes the water in their pee too.

Tortoises in the Mojave Desert get most of their water from eating juicy plants. But it only rains enough for those plants to grow every other year or so. How does the desert tortoise get enough water?

It saves its urine. The tortoise stores that *LIQUID GOLD*—up to one-third of its body weight—in its bladder. Then, when needed, the water in its pee flows back into the tortoise's body while the waste stays put.

Camels don't actually store water in their **HUMPS.** When they need to, they keep most of the water in their bodies from becoming pee instead. As a result, their urine becomes twice as salty as seawater. And when they do let go of it, they pee all over their legs. This helps cool them down.

As soon as they find more water, they fill up. Camels can gulp down 25 gallons of it within ten minutes.

PEE POSTINGS

Animals can't read newspapers or use cell phones. So they have to find other ways to communicate. Some use pee to **GET THEIR MESSAGE ACROSS.**

Lots of male animals pee on the edges of their territory. It's their way of saying, "Keep out, unless you want to fight!" Cats and wolves do it; white rhinos too. In fact, that's one reason dogs keep sniffing the trees in their neighborhood.

This message to "stay away" may help save Africa's wild dogs. As their own territory gets

smaller, these animals are wandering onto farms looking for food. Scientists have sprinkled **WILD DOG URINE** at the edges of the farms. They are making a pee fence, telling the dogs to stay away from angry farmers with shotguns.

Cave rats mark their territory too; they make urine trails throughout the deep caverns they call home. This time, the pee isn't telling others to keep out. It's a **STINKY ROADMAP** that tells the rats how to find their way in the dark.

The South American degu also uses pee to mark its passageways, but smell has nothing to do with it. The urine of this little rodent reflects ultraviolet light, a kind of light we cannot see. Luckily the degu can, so it has **SECRET PEE PATHS** that few other animals can detect.

The Siberian chipmunk uses someone else's pee to send a message—a misleading one. These chipmunks douse themselves with snake pee whenever they can. Smelling like a **SNAKE** (and not a tasty chipmunk) can keep other predators away.

RATS!

WAR AND PEES

Male **HIPPOS** spend a lot of time patrolling their stretch of the Nile River. Sometimes they meet up and have a border war. The hippos turn so they are butt-to-butt. They cover each other with a pee-and-poop combination, twirling their tails like propellers to get plenty at **NOSE LEVEL.** Then they move on, happy to have fought the battle.

Male lobsters **FACE** each other when they decide who rules the ocean floor. Crunching claws are only part of the scuffle. Lobsters' bladders are in their heads, and when they fight, they squirt each other in the face with pee. The loser remembers the smell of his opponent's urine. If they meet up again within a week, just a whiff of that pee tells the losing lobster to back down before he begins.

When lobsters are interested in love, not war, it's the **FEMALE** that makes the first move. She marches over and pees into a male's den, delivering a chemical **LOVE LETTER** that says, "I'm interested." Most likely he is too, so he rushes out and invites her in.

Using pee to conduct both war *and* romance does seem odd at first. But if you think about it, the pee is just announcing, "Hey, pay attention to me!"

The **BILLY GOAT** makes sure no one with a nose could miss him. He urinates on his belly and chest, even his beard. He enjoys the smell of his pee perfume and so, he hopes, will all the she-goats nearby.

A male porcupine sprays his perfume in a different direction. After a little **NOSE-RUBBING** with his lady friend, he douses her with pee. It's an unusual way to be romantic but, if you're a porcupine, **HUGGING** is not an option.

ON YOUR MARK...

NATURE'S GOLD MINE

We call it a **WASTE PRODUCT** but . . .

Hunters daub themselves and their dogs with fake raccoon pee to hide their scent from prey.

In winter, some park managers spray their beautiful evergreens with fox pee. The smell is barely noticeable outdoors. But if Christmas-tree thieves ignore the posted signs and bring them inside warm houses, the stink is overwhelming.

What else can you do with a splash of pee? Plenty.

A British bus company uses sheep urine to reduce **CITY SMOG.** A chemical in the pee converts part of fuel exhaust to nonpolluting nitrogen and steam.

People have used pee to remove ink spots. But it can help stain things too. Some cultures mixed pee with coal dust to make dye for their **TATTOOS.** Others used it while dying cotton because it helped colors like the indigo blue of blue jeans stay in the fabric.

People have used pee to cure tobacco.

They have bathed in it to cure their rheumatism.

Some cheese makers used to add a dash to their wares to create a **TANGY FLAVOR.**

AND THAT'S NOT ALL. . . .

PEE P. I.

Pee can be **A CLUE** that solves mysteries. Right now scientists are teaching mice to sniff out the fifty genes in human pee and sweat that make each person smell different from all others. Identifying someone's "odortype" could be a great way to solve crimes. Who needs a witness if a crook leaves his scent behind?

So pee may crack some mysteries, but it has helped create others. Ancient Roman spies used pee as **INVISIBLE INK** to write secrets between the lines of their official documents. (That's where the expression "Read between the lines" came from.) These messages appeared only when heated.

Pee was still part of the **SPY GAME** a few decades ago. A U.S. agent stood in front of a sink washing his hands, waiting for President Brezhnev of the Soviet Union to walk in the restroom. The spy signaled which stall the president used, and fellow spies drained that pipe after the flush. They examined Brezhnev's pee to find out about his health.

URINE THE ARMY NOW

Huge armies create huge amounts of waste. **GETTING RID OF IT** can be a big job. Sometimes it's better if they don't. . . .

During the Civil War, the Confederacy needed a chemical called saltpeter to make **GUNPOWDER.** The South didn't have mines where saltpeter could be found, but they did have pee. And a way to make saltpeter out of human urine. So the army put ads in the newspaper asking Southern ladies to save their pee. It also said that "wagons with barrels will be sent around to gather up the lotion."

During World War I, soldiers used their own

pee. In April 1915, the German army released poison gas as a weapon for the first time. By May, the Allied armies had invented the first **GAS MASKS.** Soldiers tied urine-soaked cloths around their noses and mouths. A chemical in their pee gave them a chance to run before the poison hurt them.

Even today pee still comes in handy. To keep soldiers from carrying too much weight into battle, the U.S. army gives them dried food in a pouch. At mealtime, soldiers must put the moisture back in. First choice, water—clean or dirty—the pouch filters out the **YUCKY STUFF.** But in a pinch, pee will do the job.

PEE M. D.

Doctors have always used urine to diagnose disease. To detect an illness called diabetes, for example, some docs poured pee onto sand to see if it attracted bugs. This idea made sense; diabetes makes urine sweet. That's why other physicians just **DIPPED A FINGER IN** and took a taste.

Today doctors in England are leaving the dirty work to others. They have discovered that some dogs can detect cancer just by smelling people's urine.

Throughout history, people have also used pee to treat illness. Ancient Greek doctors tried curing **MADNESS** with donkey pee. Others tried to get rid of fevers by boiling an egg in the patient's urine and burying it in an anthill.

American pioneers treated earaches by pouring warm urine in their ears and plugging them up with cloth.

Urine really can clean wounds and help prevent infections. Many years ago, part of a **SWORDSMAN'S NOSE** was sliced off at a duel. A doctor snatched it up, peed on it, and sewed it right back on. The nose healed perfectly.

People still use urine as medicine today. What should you do if you're in the ocean and get stung by a jellyfish? Come to shore and pee on the sting. Urine keeps the venom from making you sick.

Millions of folks in Germany, South America, and Asia use this liquid to treat more than jellyfish stings. They drink a glass of their own pee each day. They think it will cure flu, cancer, even baldness.

But the African country of Cameroon doesn't like the idea. In Cameroon, pee-drinking is a crime that can put you in *JAIL.*

PEE SOAP

Nowadays people think of urine as something to wash away, but pee was actually one of our **FIRST SOAPS.** When urine mixes with air, part of it turns into ammonia—an ingredient in many detergents on grocery store shelves.

The Pilgrims didn't have supermarkets in their America, so they made **CHAMBER LYE** instead. They let their pee sit in a barrel and then mixed it with ashes. On washday, the ammonia in their chamber lye cut through greasy stains. Another chemical in the pee acted like bleach, making clothes bright and clean. Don't worry, the Pilgrims **RINSED.**

Up in the Arctic, there is barely enough fuel to cook food, let alone melt snow to clean **SEAL BLUBBER** off the dinner dishes. So after a meal, some people used to pee into the dishpan to produce the hot "water" needed to wash up.

Other people have used pee to wash themselves. The Inuit cleaned up in steam baths made by peeing on hot rocks in enclosed tents. And in parts of India and East Africa where water is scarce or polluted, people still bathe in cow urine.

A few centuries ago, the ladies of England and France loved the way urine gave their skin a **FRESH GLOW.** Many of them peed on their hands to soften them. Others used puppy pee instead.

Here in the United States of the twenty-first century, we don't pee on our hands—except by mistake. Instead, we let laboratories pull the **MAGIC INGREDIENT** out of urine that smoothes and moistens our skin. Then, when it's safely called "urea," we put it into our creams and lotions.

PEE SOUP

The Chinook Indian tribe used to make **"CHI-NOOK OLIVES"** by soaking acorns in pee for five months. European bakers used pee to help their bread rise before they discovered yeast. And some Africans still mix cow urine into their milk.

Butterflies sip nectar from flowers, but they flutter over to pee-soaked leaves and puddles any chance they get. Urine is a butterfly's best source of **VITAMINS.**

Reindeer love the stuff because they don't have many other ways to get salt. In fact, when Siberian men want to catch their reindeer to hook them up to their sleds, they just go outside and unfasten their pants. The reindeer rush right over.

The Inuit used to catch wild reindeer by covering the top of a pit with thin slabs of ice. Then they would pee in a line leading up to the trap and add a couple of **EXTRA SPLASHES** on top. The reindeer couldn't believe their good luck—until they fell into the pit.

During their long months of hibernation, bears don't pee at all. They **RECYCLE.** Their bodies convert their pee into protein and use it as food.

WEE BEASTIES

Skin softener, heart medicine, a weapon in the battle against global warming—pee is clearly a help to us throughout our lives. But did you know that its usefulness begins even before we are born?

While we grow in our mothers' bellies, we **FLOAT** in a sac of fluid. As we get bigger, the sac gets bigger and the amount of liquid doubles. Toward the end of our time in there, most of that liquid is urine.

HEY, WE HAD TO PEE SOMEWHERE.

And it's good that we did; this pee helped us grow. We swallowed it and peed it out, over and over again. It exercised our lungs and windpipes so we could eat and breathe for the rest of our lives.

Clearly this was a very important routine. But it's no wonder we're ready to get out of there after nine months!

AFTERWORD: THE PEE REPORT

I really enjoyed writing *The Truth About Poop,* and it seemed as if many kids enjoyed reading it. When the idea of writing *Gee Whiz!* first came up, I wanted to be sure there was enough amazing information to fill it.

I got to work. I found a book called *Clean and Decent* that explained Leonardo da Vinci's love of spiral staircases (page 92) and his invention of a folding toilet seat. Fun. I read *The Bath Room,* where I learned about what the Roman government did with the pee from its public toilets (page 90). Incredible. Once I went online and discovered the Confederacy's use for pee during the Civil War (page 118), I knew I'd found a gold mine.

As always, talking to experts supplied fabulous facts. Dr. Jeffrey L. Forgeng of Higgins Armory Museum explained how knights peed while in their armor, but suggested their best choice was to plan ahead. Veterinarian Sara Levine told me about how developing chicks pee in their eggshells. Then she mentioned Farley Mowat, a man who studied wolves and peed

around the edges of his own camp to see what the wolves would do (they peed on top of the markings he made!). And Gary Uhl, Director of Design for American Standard Companies, predicted that, in the future, American showers and bathtubs will be in different rooms from toilets. Small toilet rooms will be scattered around our houses, some even scaled down to kid-sized.

RESEARCH IS FUN! Try your own and learn more about this subject by looking at:

- *Grossology* by Sylvia Branzei, published by Price Stern Sloan, 2002.
- *Oh, Yuck! The Encyclopedia of Everything Nasty* by Joy Masoff, published by Workman Publishing Company, 2000.
- *The Wee Book of Pee* by Kelly Regan Barnhill, published by Capstone Press, 2009.

Or visit the website **www.theplumber.com**.

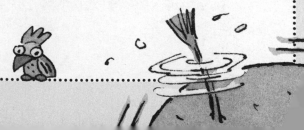

STOP LOOKING UP. DESPITE POPULAR BELIEF, AIRPLANES DO NOT FLUSH "BLUE ICE"——THE CONTENTS OF THEIR TOILETS——OUT INTO THE AIR. IT GOES INTO TANKS THAT CAN ONLY BE OPENED WHEN PLANES ARE ON THE GROUND. • IN COLONIAL AMERICA, WET BABY DIAPERS (KNOWN AS "NAPKINS") WEREN'T ALWAYS WASHED BETWEEN USES BUT WERE JUST PUT BY THE FIRE TO DRY. • MICE CAN RECOGNIZE THEIR ELDERS BY THE SMELL OF THEIR PEE. • ESKIMOS USED TO USE A BUNCH OF GRASS THAT HAD BEEN WETTED WITH URINE TO CLEAN THEIR MOUTHS AFTER EATING. • MOUSE PEE IS SO STINKY, SCIENTISTS BUILT A SPECIAL MOUSE HOUSE SO ASTRONAUTS COULD BRING MICE INTO SPACE. THE UNIT CAN CONTROL THE ODORS FOR TWENTY-ONE DAYS. TO BE SAFE, NASA ONLY ALLOWS MICE UP THERE FOR SEVENTEEN. • CRANE OPERATORS BUILDING SKYSCRAPERS CAN'T CLIMB DOWN HUNDREDS OF FEET TO PEE. EACH MORNING THEY GO INTO THEIR CABINS WITH A LUNCH PAIL AND A DIFFERENT KIND OF BUCKET. THEY SPEND THEIR DAY EMPTYING ONE AND FILLING THE OTHER. • ZOOKEEPERS IN CALCUTTA, INDIA, WERE CAUGHT DRUGGING RHINOS TO MAKE THEM PEE MORE. THEY SOLD THE URINE TO PEOPLE FOR MEDICINE. • IN 1669, HENNIG BRANDT DISCOVERED PHOSPHORUS, THE THIRTEENTH ELEMENT, WHILE DOING EXPERIMENTS WITH URINE. • SCIENTISTS ARE GENETICALLY ALTERING MICE SO THEY CAN GROW HUMAN DRUGS IN THEIR BLADDERS AND PEE IT OUT. • PEOPLE WHO WORK OUTSIDE, LIKE FISHERMEN AND LUMBERJACKS, SOMETIMES PEE ON THEIR HANDS TO WARM THEM. • IN AFRICA, FARMERS

SPRAY COW PEE ON COTTON PLANTS, AND IT KEEPS THE BUGS AWAY. IF IT DRIPS INTO THE SOIL, IT WORKS AS FERTILIZER TOO. • ROMANS USED URINE AS A MOUTH-WASH AND TOOTH CLEANER. • IN JAPAN, URINE USED TO BE SOLD TO FARMERS TO BE MADE INTO FER-TILIZER. • IN ANCIENT MEXICO, AZTEC DOCTORS HAD PATIENTS DRINK URINE TO RELIEVE STOMACH PROB-LEMS. • SOME OF THE WORDS FOR TOILET INCLUDE THE CAN, JOHN, FLUSHER, HEAD, LATRINE, POT, THRONE, DOINGS, NECESSARIUM, AND THE HOLY OF HOLIES. • WOMEN TAKE THREE TIMES AS LONG IN THE BATH-ROOM AS MEN. • A JAPANESE COMPANY HAS CREATED A TOILET THAT PLAYS ONE OF SIX SOUNDTRACKS WHEN IN USE, INCLUDNG RUSHING WATER AND BIRDSONG. • URINE HELPS CONTRIBUTE TO GREENHOUSE GASES, SO THE NEW ZEALAND GOVERNMENT WANTED TO TAX FARMERS FOR EACH COW AND SHEEP THEY OWNED. THE LAW DIDN'T PASS. • IN ONE VOODOO CURSE, A BOTTLE IS FILLED WITH PINS, NEEDLES, NAILS, "EVIL" HERBS, AND THE VICTIM'S URINE; THEN IT'S WEDGED IN A HOLE IN A TREE WHERE IT CAN'T BE FOUND. THE VICTIM IS SUPPOSED TO GET KIDNEY DISEASE. • MALE ELEPHANTS FIND OUT IF A FEMALE IS IN THE MOOD FOR ROMANCE BY SNIFFING HER PEE. • IN THE SIXTEENTH CENTURY, THE ENGLISH AND DUTCH USED TO "DRINK FLAPDRAGONS"— TOAST SOMEONE'S HEALTH BY DRINKING URINE. • IN BRAZIL, IN 1963, LONGSHOREMEN WENT ON STRIKE FOR 20 PERCENT "SHAME PAY" WHEN THEY HAD TO UNLOAD TOILETS.